# Quick Start Guide
# to Affiliate Marketing

*Answers to the Questions You*
*Should Be Asking*

# Contents

# Dedication

I dedicate this book to the person who may never grasp the ins and outs of performance marketing, but whose life path has become the best example of hard work translated into performance and success – hers, her children's, her grandchildren's, and already great-grandchildren's too.

*To my grandmother, Lidiya N. Bezobrazova*

# Preface

I can't count how many times I have been asked to write a book for affiliates. In the course of the past 7 years I have authored two bestselling volumes on affiliate program management, but also dozens of magazine articles and well over a thousand blog posts – a good number of which, in fact, were written for affiliates. So, I decided to sit down and write an actual book for affiliates as well.

# Acknowledgements

I would like to acknowledge the support of Misty Popovich for watching over my English. I also thank everyone who expressed their excitement upon hearing the news of this book being "in the works," including my littlest (but, nonetheless, the greatest! as she seemed to be more excited than anyone else) encourager – my precious daughter.

# Foreword

I started my first online marketing agency at the dawn of the commercial Internet. Everything that we did was breaking new ground. There were no rules. Instead, there was a lot of hype and enthusiasm. There was also a sense of euphoria as visionary individuals and smaller companies ushered in a new connected era from the grass roots level. Similarly to all of the technological revolutions that came before it, the early days of the Internet were characterized by unfettered innovation followed by consolidation. Dot Com start-ups with unsustainable business models imploded and took billions of venture capital investor dollars with them. The Internet has since matured a bit, and grownups are again running the show. Large companies with big budgets for driving online traffic are often dominating the scene.

However, there is still a devoted core of innovators living among the nooks and crannies of this new fiber-optic jungle. These people are restless. They are not afraid of risk. They are willing to reinvent themselves on a continual basis. And they put their money where their mouth is. These "affiliates" are willing to get paid only if they produce results by driving sign-ups or actual sales to a website. They spend their time and financial resources in order to uncover hidden opportunities, and in the process create income streams for themselves.

My digital agency had been running large-scale pay-per-click campaigns for our clients, just as the affiliate industry was exploding. We typically managed pay-per-click campaigns based on a percentage of the media budget spent. Unfortunately we were not being compensated based on the true value of what we were creating. One day we realized that we could make more money by also signing up for affiliate programs. We started to buy pay-per-click traffic with our own money and aim it at high-value affiliate offers that we thought would pay off. This led us to also improve the landing pages to which we were sending the traffic and SiteTuners was born. SiteTuners has since become a leading agency for conversion rate optimization (CRO) - helping large and small companies to improve the efficiency of their websites and landing pages.

During our own super-affiliate odyssey we made a lot of money. We also took our lumps in the process, and learned many lessons the hard way. There were unexpected and unwelcome surprises at every step, because we were blazing our own path. I wish I had had an experienced mentor back then who would have saved us much of the pain, time, and lost financial opportunity; unfortunately there was no one.

You, dear reader, are more fortunate! Geno Prussakov is an intelligent and experienced guide to this untamed affiliate marketing landscape. All of his lessons are grounded in direct experience that has been battle-tested in the real world. He has managed affiliate programs for top companies like Forbes and Skype, as well as hundreds of smaller firms. He is a noted expert speaker, writer, and founder of the Affiliate Management Days international conference series. I am also proud to call him my friend. The bottom line is that you could not ask for a better person to quickly show you the essentials of affiliate marketing.

Read this book before your competitors do, and put it into action to create your own financial freedom!

TIM ASH
CEO of SiteTuners
Chair of Conversion Conference
Author of the bestselling book *Landing Page Optimization*

# Introduction

No, this book won't make you rich quickly. Being an avid fishing fan, I am a big believer in distributing fishing *tackle* and tips (*knowledge*), not the fish itself. Therefore, what this book *will* do is walk you through the key affiliate marketing notions, answering the most important questions, and equipping you with the information you need in order to chart your own road map for affiliate success.

For ease of use I have decided to follow a question and answer format, putting together a reference book that does not have to be read successively. You may flip it open on the page that addresses your specific question, and quickly find the answer to it.

This book consists of three main parts:
1. The Basics
2. Getting Started & Day-to-Day Work
3. Advanced Topics

Altogether, in these three parts I have answered 60 questions, the vast majority of which are geared toward aspiring affiliates as well as people exploring the opportunity of making money "selling other people's stuff."

There is also an appendix that follows the main body of the book, providing you with a *Glossary of Affiliate Marketing Abbreviations* you need to know.

Committing to study/cover just 20 questions a day, you should have this whole book completed in three days. Enjoy the read, and do not hesitate to contact me with any questions at geno@amnavigator.com or via Twitter at @ePrussakov.

I am also available to conduct workshops and welcome speaking opportunities.

# I.
# The Basics

## What is affiliate marketing?

Affiliate marketing is simply performance-based marketing, whereby affiliates promote a merchant's product and/or service and get remunerated for every sale, visit, or subscription sent to the merchant. The most frequently used payment arrangements include: pay-per-sale, pay-per-lead, and pay-per-click compensations (more below).

Per Forrester Consulting the affiliate marketing spending in the USA is nearing $3 billion in 2013 and is set to reach $4.5 billion by 2016. According to a 2013 PriceWaterhouseCoopers / IABUK study in the UK affiliate marketing contributes to some 100 million transactions and 70 million leads annually, accounting for 7-9% of UK online marketing spend; and 0.6% of the country's GDP (or nearly as much as agriculture).

Affiliate marketing owes its birth and first developments to CDNow.com and Amazon.com. Back in November, 1994 CDNow started its Buyweb Program – the first online marketing program of its kind at the time. Amazon continued this pattern in July 1996 with its Associates Program. Amazon claims that currently the number of their affiliates worldwide exceeds 1 million associates.

There are different ways to run, manage and promote affiliate programs, which may involve multiple parties in the relationship, but the two main participants (without which the existence of the very marketing channel would've not been possible) are: (a) the party that has the product (or service), and (b) the party that knows how to sell it. The former is the *merchant* (sometimes also called "advertiser"), while the latter is the *affiliate* (sometimes called "publisher"). In this book we will focus on the latter.

Years ago I ran an online contest for the best definition of affiliate marketing. Chris Sanderson of AMWSO who ended up winning the first prize summarized things both eloquently and beautifully – he defined affiliate marketing as "the art of doing a merchant's marketing better than they can, and profiting from it." Many successful affiliates (also frequently called *super affiliates* in the U.S.) are truly better experts in what they do than most of the merchants that they promote. Consequently, they can market online merchant's products/services in such a way that merchants get incremental business, while they themselves make a good living off the affiliate payouts that they receive in return.

## What is an affiliate?

When looking at how the term is defined in any literature on business and economics, it is easy to be misled. Here are just a few classic definitions:

- *Compilation of State and Federal Privacy Laws* tells us that the term "means any company that controls, is controlled by, or is under common control with another company" (Privacy Journal, 2002).
- Michael R. Lavin in his *Business Information* points out that the term "can be used as a generic word to indicate either a subsidiary or division (Oryx Press, 1992).
- Arvind V. Phatak in his *International Dimensions of Management* writes that terms such as *affiliate* and *subsidiary* should be (and are) "used synonymously" (Dame Publishing, 1994).
- Finally, in their *Security Analysis: Principles and Technique* volume, the infamous Benjamin Graham and David Dodd make an observation that *affiliate* is more indefinite that *subsidiary*. They write that "an affiliate may be a company effectively controlled — perhaps jointly with others — though ownership is less than 50%. Or the relationship may exist through control of both companies by the

same owning group or 'parent', with resultant close commercial or operating ties." Also, "in some cases a company may be called an affiliate although it really is a subsidiary." (McGraw-Hill, 2005)

However, *none* of the above come even close to what the term "affiliate" means in the context of affiliate marketing! Looking at the mentions of common ownership, control, and "close commercial or operating ties," we can conclude that one "affiliate" can almost be an antonym of the other. Neither of these elements is present in the context of affiliate-merchant relationship (in performance marketing contexts).

Affiliates, as the term is being used throughout this book and in online marketing, are independent marketers who may choose to promote a business, and be paid on performance-based basis. Say one has an online storefront where they sell the crafts they produce. They may start an affiliate program whereby they would pay everyone who sends them a sale a percentage of that sale. They then become an advertiser (often also called merchant), while those who refer sales to them are their affiliates (frequently also called publishers).

As mentioned above, affiliates are *independent* marketers who choose what affiliate programs to promote, and what programs to drop, what merchants to push more aggressively, and on what merchants to spend less effort. They are self-managed and not accountable to merchants for performance. All of this makes them very different from the traditional business definition of an "affiliate."

## How much do affiliates earn?

Having surveyed more than 1,600 the 2013 Affiliate Summit AffStat Report arrived at the following distribution of "annual income derived from affiliate marketing efforts" (p. 23):

- 39.9% - less than $5,000
- 11.8% - $5,000 to $9,999
- 13.1% - $10,000 to $24,999
- 5.9% - $25,000 to $49,999
- 9.2% - $50,000 to $99,999
- 2.0% - $100,000 to $199,999
- 2.0% - $200,000 to $299,999
- 2.0% - $300,000 to $399,999
- 2.0% - $400,000 to $499,999
- 3.3% - more than $500,000
- 9.8% - "would rather not say"

As the above data shows, affiliate marketing may end up being anything from your casual earnings to a sustainable income, though only 17% of the respondents said their affiliate marketing income nears or exceeds a U.S. median annual salary. Additionally, the following two examples may inspire you further.

In late 2009 the following Tweet caught my eye:

**Scott Silverman**
@scottsilverman

Over $450K has been raised this year for the Ray Greenly Scholarship Fund via Cybermonday.com. I think Ray would be very proud!

Reply    Retweet    Favorite    More

11:14 AM - 16 Dec 09

Source: https://twitter.com/scottsilverman/status/6734340333

Knowing that CyberMonday.com was an affiliate website (owned by the National Retail Federation) I went on to dig deeper into this. Upon looking at their traffic figures, I learned that with an average January-September 2009 traffic of some 13,000 visitors, CyberMonday.com saw a jump to 95,000 in October, and a huge spike to over 2,000,000 visitors in November. It was mid-December when I analyzed their traffic statistics, but even at that stage it was obvious that one can do very well with a niche holiday-oriented website (clearly, most of their $450,000 affiliate commissions were earned in the course of November).

As I was working on this book, a famous Australian blogger, author, speaker, Darren Rowse (also known as ProBlogger) put together an interesting post. Celebrating his 10 years with Amazon's Associates Program, he created *The Ultimate Guide to Making Money with the Amazon Affiliate Program*. In it he disclosed his (USD) earnings as an Amazon affiliate over the course of his 10 years with them:

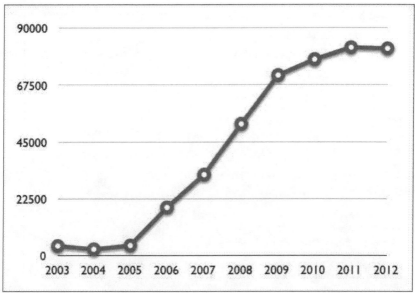

Source: http://www.problogger.net/archives/2013/04/24/the-ultimate-guide-to-making-money-with-the-amazon-affiliate-program/

In April of 2013, Darren wrote: "Overall I estimate my Amazon earnings, since 2003, are around the $420,000 mark (USD) – although, as you can see, the bulk of it has been in the last 5-6 years." As you can see from the above-referenced chart, this content affiliate has been steadily making between $70,000 and $80,000 a year from one affiliate program.

Between AffStat's numbers and these two examples you should get a good idea of what affiliates earn. Don't set the wrong expectations though – the megabucks one often expects to make via affiliate marketing are often being earned for a smaller percentage, and take some time and effort to make.

### What consumer actions do affiliates get paid for?

As you already know from the above answers, you can get paid *per sale* and *per lead*. In the former case, it may either be a percentage of the order value (where the shipping cost is normally excluded), or a fixed amount per sale. In case with leads, it is generally a flat amount per lead. However, affiliate marketing employs many more than just these two payment models. Here is more detailed look (with corresponding abbreviations):

- PPC – **Pay Per Click** – An Internet marketing model in which website owners pay only for targeted *clicks*. Due to high vulnerability to fraud, very few advertisers use this model today. The only noteworthy example is eBay Partner Network.
- PPL – **Pay Per Lead** – A model in which payment is due only when qualifying *leads* are received by the advertiser. Alternative abbreviation: CPL (Cost Per Lead).
- PPS – **Pay Per Sale** – An Internet marketing model in which payment is due only when qualifying *sales*

are received by the advertiser/merchant. Alternative abbreviation: CPS (Cost Per Sale).

- PPCall – **Pay Per Call** – A marketing payment model where remuneration is due when qualifying *calls* are received by the advertiser. This model is frequently used by merchants in conjunction with one (or several) of the above three.

You want to also be aware of such models as PPV (pay per *view*) and PPI (pey per *install*). However, due to their frequent association with unwanted activity (adware and spyware), I do not recommend looking beyond the above-quoted four models. In fact, since very few merchants pay for clicks these days, PPL, PPS and PPCall would be the three I would focus on.

### Will my income be 100% passive?

You'll certainly hear the phrase often. However, if by "passive income" you imply fully automated earnings that don't require your ongoing involvement, I have to disappoint you. You may indeed automate many things as an affiliate. However, due to the dynamic and constantly evolving nature of Internet marketing, it is not possible to build a 100% secure passive income stream. You will have to put time (and effort) into it.

### What is an affiliate program?

An affiliate program is a business arrangement whereby one party (the merchant) agrees to pay another party (the affiliate) based on any of the above-quoted models. The payment is remitted for all the actions that occur in the event of the end customer clicking the affiliate link which leads to the merchant's website, and thus, results in a purchase or a lead. For the sake of clarity, it is important to emphasize that the money is paid on all *confirmed* (and *valid*) leads or orders.

In rare instances affiliate programs are also called associate, reseller, commission, revenue-sharing, bounty, or partnership programs.

### What types of affiliates exist out there?

Since affiliate marketing is a marketing context (not a "channel" or a type of marketing), it can work with, virtually, all types and channels of online marketing. The ten more widely spread types of affiliates would encompass:

i. **Content** affiliates – those producing their own online content or encouraging user-generated content. Examples: Answers.com, About.com

ii. **Coupon** affiliates – those aggregating and distributing coupon and/or voucher codes and, discounts. Examples: RetailMeNot, Offers.com

iii. **Data feed** affiliates – those creating websites using advertisers' product and/or offer feeds. Examples: Pronto.com, Shopzilla, TheFind.com

iv. **Display** affiliates – those that market using display advertising. Examples: Forbes.com, SmallBizTrends.com

v. **Email** affiliates – those that market via email

vi. **Loyalty** affiliates – sometimes also called "incentive affiliates" they encourage the desired end-user action by such incentives as cashback/rebates, points, miles, virtual currency, etc. Examples: BigCrumbs.com, TopCashBack.co.uk

vii. **Mobile** affiliates – those that utilize mobile marketing methods (from specific campaigns to apps) to drive the desired action. Example: the above-mentioned TheFind.com has a mobile app

viii. **SEM** affiliates – those that use their SEO and/or PPC marketing skills to drive targeted traffic (and conversions) to advertisers' websites

ix. **Social Media** affiliates – those that utilize social media channels (e.g.: Twitter, Facebook) in their marketing

x. **Video** affiliates – those that actively employ online video marketing

Naturally, the more successful affiliates use several of the above types of promotion in their marketing mix.

### How does one get started?

Since prior to approving you into their affiliate program most merchants will want to review your website, to plug into the affiliate marketing world you will want to first start a website (a basic content website, like a blog, would be the easiest way to start), and only then open affiliate accounts on major affiliate networks, and with in-house-based affiliate programs.

### What are the startup costs?

No worthwhile affiliate program (or affiliate network) will charge you anything to become their affiliate. Therefore, starting up can be a rather low-cost exercise. As mentioned above, you will need a website. It will cost you under $10 a year to register a domain name. After that, on the minimal budget, your only ongoing expense will be the cost of website hosting (under $10 a month).

## Can I be an affiliate without a website?

While most affiliate programs will require a website (for approval), technically, one may be an affiliate without a site. For example, you could (a) run paid search campaigns linking your ads through affiliate links directly to merchants' websites, or (b) employ email marketing, or (c) work via the above-mentioned pay-per-call model which works even offline. However, it is always a good idea to still have a website where you will explain/list the marketing methods that you use (many merchants will not even consider your application if you do not have a site); and always double-check with each individual affiliate program if your "websiteless" methods are okay with the merchant. Do it *before* applying into an affiliate program. It is always better to have clarity on things like these before your commissions are reversed (because your methods turned out to be incompatible with the merchant's strategy for its affiliate program).

## What time investment are we talking about?

You can invest as little or as much time as you are ready to. It can be anything from a couple of hours a week, to 1-2 hours a day, to a full working day (when you are, finally, in a position to quit your "day job"). Just remember to take it one step at a time and not jump into the river without thoroughly educating yourself about the underwater "surprises."

## How technically savvy do I have to be?

While coders and programmers do have certain advantages over pure right-brain marketers, you do not *have to be* tech-savvy to become successful in affiliate marketing. I am not. Yes, programming skills can help, but you may

**19**

always outsource the work, or use tools (like the data feed and/or coupon integration tools that we will discuss later in the book).

### May I promote more than one merchant from the same niche?

Absolutely! As a free marketer, you are the one who chooses the merchants into which you are going to invest your effort. Merchants know this, and in the course of all my time in affiliate marketing, I have *never* seen a merchant who requests, not to mention requires, exclusivity.

### What affiliate platforms should I be aware of?

As I have already alluded to above, affiliate programs can be divided into two main types: those run on *affiliate networks* (e.g.: BestBuy.com runs their program on Commission Junction, Walmart.com's affiliate program is based on LinkShare, ToysRUs.com's program is supported by eBay Enterprise Affiliate Network, while Under Armour's affiliate program is on AvantLink) and those run on *in-house* platforms (e.g.: Amazon.com, eBay, BettyMills). The commonly-used industry lingo for an in-house program is "indie."

### What exactly is an affiliate network?

Affiliate networks are essentially mediators connecting affiliates with affiliate programs, providing tracking, reporting and maintenance services both to merchants (i.e. those who run affiliate programs), and to affiliates. In merchant-affiliate relationships, affiliate networks are also the ones who pay affiliates (helping you aggregate payments across different affiliate programs, streamlining the payment process for both parties involved).

## What affiliate networks are available?

Affiliate networks are numerous. Below you will find a geographically categorized list. The list arranges affiliate networks strictly in an alphabetical order, not necessarily in order of any personal preference. It is also not my goal to publish a comprehensive list of affiliate networks. What I have done is my best to bring to you the world's major networks currently in operation:

**NORTH AMERICAN AFFILIATE NETWORKS**

AffiliateFuture

Affiliate Window

AvantLink

Avangate

ClickBank

Commission Junction

eBay Enterprise Affiliate Network

Impact Radius (multichannel affiliate network)

LinkConnector

LinkShare

oneNetworkDirect

OfferMobi (mobile affiliate network)

ShareASale

ShareResults

Video Performance Network (video)

Webgains US

Zanox.com

**SOUTH AMERICAN AND HISPANIC TARGETING NETWORKS**

7reach.com (Argentina & Brasil)

Adverlatin

Batanga Network

Filiado.com

Fox Netwoks

Harren Media

MediaCom (Brasil)

**UK AFFILIATE NETWORKS**

Advertising.com

Advortis

Affiliate Advantage

Affiliate Window

AffiliateFuture UK

AffiliNet

Afform

Ocean Affiliate

OffersQuest

OMG Network

Paid On Results

Profitistic

QwertyTrade.com

R O Eye

clixGalore
Commission Junction UK
DGM-UK.com
GlobalDirectMedia.com
LinkShare UK
Netklix

SilverTap
SmartQuotes
TML Affiliate
TradeDoubler.co.uk
Webgains UK
Zanox.co.uk

### FRENCH AFFILIATE NETWORKS
Advertising.com
Commission Junction France
MobPartner (mobile)
Netaffiliation
OMGfr.com

PublicIdees
TradeDoubler
Webgains
Zanox

### GERMAN AFFILIATE NETWORKS
Advertising.com
Affili.net
Belboon.com
CommissionJunction.de
OMGde.com

Sponsormob (mobile)
SuperClix
TradeDoubler
Webgains
Zanox

### SCANDINAVIAN AFFILIATE NETWORKS
7reach.com (Denmark)
Advertising.com (Denmark, Norway, Sweden)
Affiliator (Sweden)
Commission Junction Sverige (Sweden)

Double.net (Sweden)
TradeDoubler (Denmark, Finland, Norway, Sweden)
Webgains (Denmark, Sweden)
Zanox (Denmark, Finland, Norway, Sweden)

### EASTERN EUROPEAN AFFILIATE NETWORKS
eHub.cz (Czech Republic)
Potenza.cz (Czech Republic)
ForestView.ru (Greece)
Linkwise (Greece & Cyprus)
Afilo (Poland)
NetSales.pl (Poland)
TradeDoubler (Poland)
Zanox (Poland)

Affiliation.ro (Romania)
2Parale.ro (Romania)
Adnations.co.uk (multiple countries)
AechMedia.com (multiple countries)
Click2Sell.eu (Lithuania)
Sworp.com (UK-based, covering Slovakia, Poland, and Czech Republic)

### RUSSIAN AFFILIATE NETWORKS
1Lead.ru
ActionAds.ru
ActionPay.ru

HIMBA.ru
Lead100.ru
LeadGid.ru

Ad1.ru
AdmitAd.com
Advaction.ru
Afrek.ru
Apelsin-1.ru
Babki-online.ru
CityAds.ru
CPANetwork.ru
CPartner.ru
DirectProfit.ru
GdeSlon.ru
HeyMoose.com

Leads.su
LeadsLeader.ru
Leadster.ru
MasterTarget.ru
MixMarket.ru
Motiv8.ru
Myragon.ru
QXPlus.ru
SellTarget.ru
TopAdvert.ru
TradeTracker.ru
Unilead.ru

## AUSTRALIAN AFFILIATE NETWORKS
CheckMyStats.com.au
clixGalore (also New Zealand)
Commission Monster

CoProsper
DarkBlue.com
dgmMarketing.com.au (also New Zealand)

## INDIAN AFFILIATE NETWORKS
AffiliateCurry
clixGalore

DGM-India.com

## ASIA-BASED AFFILIATE NETWORKS
8Affiliate.com
AccessTrade.net (Japan)
AdForBest.com
Alimama (China)
Allyes.com (China)
AsiaClickz
Baidu Union (China)
Chinese AN (China, Hong Kong, Taiwan)

ClickValue.cn (China)
clixGalore (Japan)
JANet (Japan)
LinkShare (Japan)
LuckyPacific.com
U2Mee.com (China)
ValueCommerce (Japan)
Zanox (Japan)

## OTHER COUNTRIES
AdsMarket.com (Israel)
Advertising.com (Spain)
OfferForge.com (South Africa)
Pay4Results.eu (multiple countries)

SprinTrade.com (Italy)

TradeDoubler (multiple European countries)
TrafficSynergy (South Africa)
Webgains (Ireland, the Netherlands, Spain)
Zanox (multiple European countries)

Each network has its own rules, regulations, and terms of service. As exemplified earlier, it isn't unusual for different online merchants to work with different affiliate networks. In the U.S., I recommend affiliates to start accounts with such major networks as (again, in alphabetical order only) Affiliate Window, AvantLink, Commission Junction, LinkShare, eBay Enterprise Affiliate Network, and ShareASale. In the United Kingdom, consider Affiliate Window, OMG, PaidOnResults, and TradeDoubler.

### Should I prefer network-based programs over "indies"?

It depends. As mentioned above, working with merchants through affiliate networks is more convenient (and especially for beginning affiliates) due to the ability to aggregate payments across numerous affiliate programs. Additionally, across-the-board reporting is also good to have. If, however, the niche you choose to work in justifies joining in-house-based affiliate programs, definitely go for it. With giants like Amazon and eBay reliability shouldn't be a problem. With smaller merchants – take it easy before you're 100% certain you won't burn yourself.

### Is it possible to have all my reporting in one place?

Certainly! There are both tools that can help you unify the reporting across different affiliate networks and merchants (like Affmeter and Affiliatereporting.com, for example), but the good ole Excel can work well too (exporting your reports from the above-discussed platforms and importing them into your own "environment").

## How exactly are payments handled?

Most affiliate networks and in-house affiliate programs either pre-set or allow affiliates to choose their payment thresholds, upon reaching which your payment is remitted. Here is a basic comparison of payment methods available across five major US affiliate networks at the time of this book's writing:

- AvantLink – Checks, direct deposits (U.S. banks only), and PayPal.
- Commission Junction – Direct deposits and checks. Direct bank deposits (ACH) available only for select countries.
- Google Affiliate Network [retired in 2013] – Paid affiliates through their AdSense accounts.
- LinkShare – Direct deposits (for select countries) and checks.
- ShareASale – Direct deposits for US, Canada, UK, and Euro-based E.U. accounts that support this payment method, and checks sent via regular mail or FedEx.

Select affiliate networks (e.g.: Avangate, MarketHealth.com, GdeSlon.ru) and affiliate programs (e.g.: eToro), also collaborate with solutions like Payoneer, which allow them to pay affiliates through personal prepaid MasterCard cards, local bank transfers, local e-wallets, and international checks.

## What are affiliate network (terms of use) agreements?

They are the agreements that govern your relationship with the affiliate network. Among other things, these agreements cover such important provisions as the terms of network's service, promotional rules and restrictions, and payment terms. Make sure you thoroughly familiarize yourself with these starting to work with an affiliate network. Keeping track (say, in an Excel table) of the specific terms of various networks is helpful too.

Below you will find links to a few terms of use agreements from select U.S. affiliate networks:

- Affiliate Window - us.affiliatewindow.com/policies
- AvantLink - www.avantlink.com/terms-conditions
- Commission Junction - www.cj.com/psa
- LinkShare - http://bit.ly/LS-ToS
- eBay Enterprise Affiliate Network - http://bit.ly/PJ-ToS
- ShareASale - www.shareasale.com/agreement.cfm

Do not underestimate the importance of these legally binding documents, and make sure you understand them -- both to comply with them, and to set your expectations on the proper level.

### What are cookies and why are they important?

Affiliate sales are normally tracked using cookies (small text files set on the visitor's computer), and the duration of how long to keep them on the visitor's machine is called the cookie life. In our context, it means the time period between the end-user's click on our affiliate link and the last day when the merchant is willing to pay us a commission on the sale made by the visitor we've referred to them.

### Are cookies the only way the affiliate traffic and conversions are tracked?

Not at all. There are a number of platforms — and by "platforms" I mean both affiliate program software, and affiliate networks — that do not depend on cookies for tracking or do not depend on cookies only. Tracking may also be tied to the shopping cart, the end-user's IP, or be URL-based (when affiliate IDs are being embedded in each URL), or incorporate a number of other "cookie-less" solutions. Such software (for in-house affiliate programs) as DirectTrack, HasOffers, Impact Radius, LinkTrust and PostAffiliatePro, as well as such affiliate networks as Affiliate Future, ClickBank, Webgains support "cookie-free" tracking.

## Should I stay away from programs with short cookie life?

The unfortunate reality is that some merchants set affiliate cookie life at extremely short periods. The "champions" here would be Sephora.com (4 hour cookie life), Toys R Us and Babies R Us, eToys.com, Miles Kimball Company, ShopNBC.com (all - 5 hours), followed by Nordstrom.com (12 hours), Enterprise.com and Chase.com (23 hours each) and even Amazon.com (24 hours). The first affiliate reaction may be: "Why even bother?!" However, if you dig deeper, you'll find out that between 85% and 91% of purchases occur either immediately or within 24 hours after the end-customer's click on an affiliate link. Combining this reality with the fact that the above-quoted brands, generally, yield higher-than-average conversion rates makes them worth your try, anyway.

Don't get me wrong, I do *not* support short cookie life (quite the contrary, actually). I am just saying that some of these programs may still be worth your effort.

## What if a customer returns the product?

If a customer returns (or exchanges) the product they ordered through your affiliate link (be it their whole order, or a part of it), the merchant adjusts the final amount or affiliate commission based on the confirmed final sale. They may also void any affiliate transaction if any of the following behaviors are registered:

*Customer Behavior*
- Payment authorization failed
- Fraudulent sale
- Returned order or unclaimed shipment
- Duplicate order
- Cancelled order

*Affiliate Behavior*
- Fraudulent transaction
- Test transaction
- Self-referral (if this is explicitly prohibited in their affiliate program agreement)

*Merchant Behavior/Circumstances*
- Test transaction
- Order non-fulfillment

To safeguard themselves from the situations of the above-quoted types, merchants set locking periods (or lock dates).

## What are affiliate program agreements and why they are important?

Similar to affiliate networks' Terms of Service these agreements define and govern your relationship, but in this case between affiliates and merchants (or advertisers). Do not confuse them for affiliate network agreements. Many merchants will have additional terms that you will have to comply with. Make sure you study these carefully before starting to promote a merchant.

In some cases merchants will summarize the key terms of the agreement in the first paragraph. In others (see image below) their affiliate network will let them bring these to you in a more digestible form.

| Policies: | |
|---|---|
| Name | Content |
| Search Campaigns - Protected SEM Bidding Keywords <br> *Keywords that publishers are prohibited from bidding on for search marketing campaigns.* | Publishers are not allowed to bid on brand terms and trademarked terms as part of the word or phrase. Protected terms include: Verizon, Verizon.com, FiOS, Verizon Online DSL |
| Search Campaigns - Recommended SEM Bidding Keywords <br> *High performing keywords that publishers are permitted to bid on for their search marketing campaigns.* | Broadband, DSL, phone service, long distance, phone, voip, internet, telephone service, broadband phone service, internet phone company, calling plans |
| Search Campaigns - Prohibited SEM Display URL Content <br> *Terms that publishers are prohibited from using in the display URLs of search marketing campaigns.* | Publishers are not permitted to use the term Verizon in the display URL. |
| Search Campaigns - Direct Linking <br> *Specify if publishers are allowed to link directly to your Web site from their search marketing campaigns.* | No |
| Search Campaigns - Special Instructions for Search Marketing Publishers <br> *These are additional usage instructions or limitations for search marketing. Advertisers may also specify any relevant sections of Special Terms and Conditions* | Please note that Verizon Broadband is a separate program from Verizon Wireless. Program terms and conditions will vary; please abide by each program's unique set of rules. |
| Web Site - Prohibited Web Site Domain Keywords <br> *Keywords that publishers are prohibited from using in the top-level domain of their Web site* | Publishers may not use Verizon branded terms or Verizon URL(s) as Publisher's URL. |
| Apply To Program | |

Verizon Broadband Services affiliate program policies on Commission Junction

However, even when there is no introductory/summarizing paragraph, or a table similar to the above-displayed one, all affiliate program agreements tend to follow a similar pattern – see an example at www.prussakov.com/ToS – and are, generally, very easy to follow.

## What is a locking period (and/or lock date)?

It is the time period that the merchants give themselves to reverse/adjust the transaction. Affiliate-referred orders can get canceled on a whole number of reasons (some of which are outlined above), but once the "locking period" has completed, or the "lock date" has come, the commission gets permanently locked in the affiliate account, and the merchant can no longer do anything to that transaction (voiding, editing, etc).

Most affiliate networks allow merchants to choose the length of time within which they want to be able to edit/void affiliate commissions (based on how quickly they can verify the validity of sales, or on their experience with returns, or whatever other reasons may influence the commission adjustment). For example, Commission Junction's default locking date is the 10th date of the following month, while on ShareASale it is the 20th date. In cases with custom locking periods, you will see situations like that in Overstock.com (rebranded into O.co not too long ago) affiliate program – where they decided to tie it to the number of days past the order placement, setting it at "60 days after the event date" (see the image below).

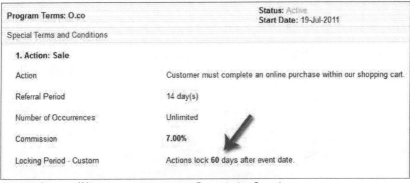

Overstock.com affiliate program terms on Commission Junction

To set your expectations right, make sure you thoroughly review the locking period information prior to applying into any affiliate program.

# II.
# Getting Started
# & Day-to-Day Work

## What are the most profitable niches?

Back in 2010 in an interview I had with the Search Engine Journal (SEJ) I was asked one of the questions that new affiliates frequently ask themselves (and others too): "Which niches are more profitable when it comes to making money as an affiliate?"

As soon as the question was asked I immediately thought of how widely-spread this misconception is — one that some niches are significantly more profitable for affiliates than others. Earlier that year addressing a similar question in an interview to Website Magazine I answered:

> Some affiliates have been led into thinking that there are "hot" products/niches in affiliate marketing (i.e. those that pay most money), but the real money is being made not on dietary supplements, or hosting. You want to (a) look at what is hot on the market at any given period of time, and monetize on those trend(s), but what is even more important: (b) establish yourself as a key player in the niche of your passion (be it music, shoes, Valentine's Day, or anything else).

In my interview to SEJ, I expanded my answer adding a word about the importance of choosing your partners carefully, and also illustrating the importance of an *all-*encompassing approach to affiliate marketing analytics. Here's that illustration:

> ... "profitable niches" should never be measured by the commission levels that are being paid by advertiser/merchant. Always look at the broader picture. Remember to look at such metrics as conversion, average order value, reversal rate, cookie life. For example, hosting companies have historically had high commission payouts (anywhere from $50 to $150 a sale, with select ones paying as much as $300-400/sale). Sounds attractive, doesn't? Well, hold your horses before you spend all of your money on those paid search ads, or advertising on other types of properties!

Hosting affiliate programs are also known to have some of the highest reversal rates in affiliate marketing history. While many affiliate networks will not disclose this piece of information to you, it is not unusual for a hosting company to reverse between 50% and 80% of all affiliate transactions...

Conversely, if you are selling a lower priced product/service through an affiliate program that pays a lower affiliate commission, but has a beautiful conversion ratio, and low reversal rate (some merchants even offer a "no affiliate reversals" policy), *that* will be your "profitable niche".

### Can I forecast my future affiliate earnings?

Quite tentatively, but yes, you can get an idea of what to expect. While the accuracy of these projections will always be highly contingent on a number of program-specific metrics (2 through 5 below), as well as on how exactly you are going to market merchants on your website, there is a number of variables to consider prior to starting out as an affiliate — metrics that will tell you how well your website may do with affiliate marketing. Consider the following five metrics:

1. **Clickthrough Rate** (CTR) — It will be dependent on (a) how targeted your traffic is, and (b) the type of linking you'll be using (banners, text links, product links, etc).

2. **Earnings Per Click** (EPC) — This metric (frequently tied to 100 clicks as also in our further calculations below), disclosed for most affiliate programs even prior to you joining them, tells you what other affiliates are already making on this program, and while it should by no means be your single criteria (because it's an average calculated across all affiliate

activity within the program), it is a good one to analyze.

3. **Average Order Value** (AOV) — Average ticket which is calculated as a sum total of all affiliate-generated orders referred over a given period of time, and then divided by the number of orders.

4. **Conversion Rate** (CR) — The click-to-sale or click-to-lead conversion rate. Analyzing a program-specific CR is easier, especially when it is publicly available to affiliates prior to joining an affiliate program (as is the case with AvantLink-based programs, for example). Analysis of vertical-specific CR is also an option, but won't be as precise.

5. **Reversal Rate** (RR) — This is the percentage of affiliate-referred transactions that get reversed by the merchant. Unfortunately, in many cases you won't be able to analyze reversal rates prior to actually joining and experimenting with an affiliate program. Some networks, however (e.g.: AvantLink and ShareASale) do provide data on this vital metric even before you sign up with an affiliate program.

In 2010 I had a marketing consultant approach me. The consultant didn't know much about affiliate marketing but had a "potential client with a blog that gets as many as 75k unique visitors and close to 200k pageviews per month." They had the same question as you now – how can one predict affiliate marketing revenue potential for a website?

Plugging all of the above-listed metrics into their scenario (publisher with some 200,000 pageviews a month), picking a real affiliate program that pays 12% commission (comm) on all sales, presupposing a very close niche match between the affiliate and the merchant, and assuming the following:

CTR = 1%
EPC = $60
AOV = $125
CR = 5%
RR = 10%

We arrive at the following calculation:

Traffic: 200,000 × 1% (CTR) = 2,000
Sales: 2,000 × 5% (CR) = 100
Earnings: 100 × $125 (AOV) * 12% (comm) – 10% (RR) = $1,350

To arrive at your personal projected EPC you will want to divide Earnings by Traffic and multiply the result by 100. So:

$1,350 / 2,000 × 100 = $67.50

Comparing our projected EPC figure to the program's actual EPC ($60), we see that we are not that far off, and our overall projection must be sufficiently plausible.

Finally, a *word of warning*: remember that things will differ drastically from merchant to merchant. So, take things easy (especially when there are investments involved) not to fall victim to your own incorrect projections.

### What types of websites are most popular?

I like the way a fellow-marketer and book author, Jim Kukral, normally addresses such questions. He points out that people go online either (i) to solve a problem, or (ii) to be entertained. Don't you love it when someone finally systematizes it so beautifully for you? Especially when it so eloquently summarizes your own experience! I've been discussing this with affiliates for years, but never in such a simple and clear form.

When you are building a website to promote merchant's products or services through an affiliate program, you want it to be a problem-solving, or an entertaining website. *Then* they will bookmark it and come again. Synergies of the entertainment and the problem-solving components also work well. A classic example would be an affiliate website that features daily updated thematic videos, and runs relevant merchants' ads on the side, or even has a "sponsor us" section where they let their visitors purchase products imported from multiple merchants' data feeds (conveniently categorized into sections, of course).

When starting to work on a new website, keep the two above purposes in mind.

## What are "thin affiliates"? (Or thoughts on creating value)

In late 2009 Microsoft's CEO, Steve Ballmer, gave CNBC an interesting interview. When asked about the competition (namely, whether too much was being made of Microsoft competing with Google on the search front, or with Apple on other fronts), he said that it is important to understand what creates the real value (of a business, project, or product) for the consumer. Ballmer stated: "the truth is, value gets created by innovation widely adopted." This brought my thoughts back to Jason Calacanis' Affiliate Summit West 2008 keynote speech (also available on YouTube now). While being infamously aggressive in his speech (which did create the resonance that he was undoubtedly hoping to create), he also brought up the subject of *value*. He rigorously spoke out against "thin affiliates", or affiliate websites that add no real value, but "pollute" the Internet. While I did disagree with much of Calacanis' verbiage, there was a great point behind his words.

As an affiliate program manager, I have to review close to a hundred different affiliate websites daily. Some of them look like this:

Typical "banner farm" affiliate website

Is having a banner/link on this website really beneficial for the merchants that are being represented here (question of *value to the merchant*)? And is visiting this website really helping the end user in some new and constructive way, substantially contributing to the pre-sale process (question of *value to the consumer*)? The answers to both questions are evident.

It's not affiliate websites like these that make super affiliates, and it's not websites like these that are being bookmarked and revisited again. Observing dozens of super affiliates getting to the heights of their success, I have not seen one that didn't do something that (i) aimed at creating an innovation, and ultimately (ii) strove for a wide adoption. There is something affiliates can learn from Ballmer's (and Calacanis') words. There are still many opportunities out there. We just need to look at things through the consumers' eyes, see the needs, turn them into opportunities, and do everything we can to come up with such solutions that would be widely and continuously adopted.

## What are "leaks"?

Affiliates should be paying special attention to these while evaluating merchants before joining their programs. A leak is, essentially, anything on the merchant's website that may lead to a course of action where the referring affiliate will not get any credit for the referral. Here are just a few commonly occurring ones:

1. Phone number (unless tracked by the merchant)
2. Live chat (same as above)
3. AdSense units
4. Affiliate links (on merchant's website, in customer newsletters, etc)
5. Links to related (aka "family") stores/websites
6. Links to other merchants
7. Links to other affiliates

Evaluate the merchant's website carefully before investing your time, money and effort into it. After all, you don't want to work for nothing.

## What makes a banner affiliate-unfriendly?

Just as "leaky" websites, banners may also be unsuitable for affiliate usage. Here are just a few things to keep in mind when evaluating advertisers' banners:

- No banner may have a phone number on it (unless the number is being dynamically replaced by a number than tracks via a pay-per-call setup). It's a leak.
- No banner should have the merchant's URL spelled out on it. Theoretically, it leaves the option for the end user to by-pass the click, and type in the URL into the address bar directly.
- The banner must have a clear call to action on it (e.g.: "Details Here", "Learn More", "Buy Now", etc). Do not assume that the end user will understand what the banner is for. Tell them what you want them to do.
- Whenever the space allows for it, the affiliate banner should attractively display a product emphasizing the main selling points.
- Avoid banners with excessive animation. Especially flee from short time intervals between frame changes in .GIF files, which makes the text on the banners too hard (if not impossible) to read.

## What criteria help evaluate an affiliate program?

In order to not get burnt, you want to choose affiliate programs wisely. While some say the choice is as simple as "promoting those who pay more," I *strongly* disagree with this simplistic approach. It can cost you a lot of money and time spent on a wrong program before you realize it was wrong in the first place.

I believe it is useful to look at every new/prospective affiliate program (or merchant) through a prism of 15 factors, keeping also in mind that not any *one* of them exists in isolation. They are always intertwined and interdependent, and your performance with any affiliate program will always depend on a variety of these variables.

### 1. Website

Start right from the merchant's website. Look at it from two angles: as a consumer and as an affiliate. As a consumer, pay attention to its ease-of-use (both overall and the checkout process, in particular), professionalism, and also see how compelling (does it have enticing calls-to-action?) it is. As an affiliate, make sure to critically check it for any "leaks," or ways for the end consumer to take a route that does not lead to commissions. Most commonly, leaks come in forms of toll free phone numbers, online chat assistants that also take orders, links to other merchants, and even AdSense units and affiliate links of their own.

### 2. Reputation/Reliability

Check the reputation of the merchant you're planning to partner with. Once again, approach the question both as a consumer and as an affiliate. As a consumer you want to go to independent review sites (these will vary from industry to industry); as an affiliate go to affiliate forums and blogs. If there *is* something you should be aware of, it should be easy enough to find.

### 3. Prices/Competitiveness

I have seen merchants create replicas of their websites, only with higher prices, to make an affiliate program with high payouts possible. I have also seen merchants increase prices on their main website -- again, to allow for a handsome affiliate commission. Techniques like these do not help you sell. Consumers, especially in our age of easy shopping comparisons, are becoming more and more savvy. They won't buy unless the merchant is truly competitive. This applies to pricing, product selection, and even the merchant's brand.

### 4. Market Saturation

Some niches are already too crowded and unless you have something of truly unique value to add into the pre-purchase process, look for a less saturated niche. Newer affiliates will find it especially hard to compete in heavily saturated niches. Take hosting, for example. It's an interesting niche with plenty of good players (and, unfortunately, equally as many less-than-kosher ones). But it is way too saturated for a new affiliate.

### 5. Commission Amount

When you put together a comparative table, which I hope you will do, this will be one of the factors you will obviously list. However, don't be too focused on this one. There are many other variables (see list below) that go into the final formula, which you want to study as well.

### 6. Commission Recurrence

Some merchants pay commission on new and unique customers only. I do not believe this to be a good practice. In the survey conducted for my *Online Shopping Through Consumers' Eyes* book, I asked consumers: "When shopping for products requiring ongoing replenishing (e.g., grocery, ink, bank checks, etc.) and receiving satisfactory service, would you still compare your retailer's offer to other offers next time you need their product?" Close to 72% replied "yes." Therefore, it is my belief that merchants that run affiliate programs should compensate every sale equally, or even offer an additional bonus for new customers, but by no means, should they limit affiliate commissions to new customers only. Yet some do, and you want to check on this prior to signing up.

### 7. Terms of Service

In an anonymous poll I asked affiliates if they actually read affiliate program agreements prior to applying into programs. The largest group (38%) said "rarely," 14% replied "sometimes," 19% "often," and only 29% replied "always." Sobering statistics! Yet elements like commission recurrence, promotion restrictions (e.g., no direct linking from paid search ads, or no use of trademarked terms in URL paths) may be found right in the merchant's TOS and shouldn't come to you as a surprise when they start cancelling your commission on "invalid" or "unqualified" sales/leads.

### 8. Cookie Life

As we've already discussed above, this is the period of time within which the merchant agrees to compensate you for the referred customer. If it is set at 24 hours and a visitor you refer purchases 25 hours past the initial referral, you will get no commission on that sale.

### 9. Conversion Rate

This is one of the most important metrics, which helps you answer a part of the "how much will I be able to earn" question. For instance, if we take a smaller merchant who is paying a 10% commission on all sales and has a 1.5% conversion, and Amazon, which is paying only 4% but has a conversion rate (CR) of some 6% (see http://prussakov.com/AvsW for the basis of this assumption), we will see the following happen on 1,000 referrals (assuming an equal average order value of $10):

> *Smaller merchant:*
> 1,000 visitors * 1.5% CR = 15 sales
> 15 * ($10 AOV * 10%) = $15.00 commission
> *Amazon.com*
> 1,000 visitors * 6% CR = 60 sales
> 60 * ($10 AOV * 4%) = $24.00 commission

As you can see, conversion plays an extremely important role in the affiliate earnings.

### 10. EPC

EPC stands for Earnings per Click, and most affiliate networks disclose this metric even before you join a network-based affiliate program. Keep in mind that in many cases the

EPC figure you see will be tied to 100 clicks sent from an average affiliate in the program to the merchant. So if you see an EPC of $27.49, know that this is the average of how much affiliates of this merchant earn on every 100 clicks they refer.

### 11. Reversal Rate

Very few affiliate networks (e.g., ShareASale and AvantLink) disclose this information upfront, and needless to say in-house programs do not either. Therefore, most frequently affiliates have to find this metric out from their own experience with the merchant. Either way, keep a close eye on this one. Basically, every 1% of the reversal rate implies 1 reversed order per each batch of 100.

### 12. Tracking/Reporting Platform

Do your homework here and ensure that you're comfortable with the tracking and reporting platform (be it an affiliate network or their in-house software) that the merchant uses. Not all platforms are created equal and not all affiliate networks stand for the same ethical principles.

### 13. Management & Approachability

Contact the merchant and affiliate program manager. See how quickly they get back with you and how detailed/to-the-point their response is. You want to partner with someone who cares about your partnership. You'll see that some merchants do not, or at least don't appear like they do.

### 14. Creatives

Whether you are relying heavily on banner creatives, deep-linked text links, or product feed, check whether the merchant is providing adequate support here as well.

### 15. Tools

Some merchants offer you a good set of basic links and banners, others offer just a homepage link and a couple of banners, while yet others offer both some basic links *and* a way for you to create your own, and not only in simple forms, but also as widgets, video, easy product feed import, and much more. If the latter are of importance to you, check if they have these.

Ultimately, remember that time spent on the preliminary due diligence will pay off in the long-term, safeguarding you from wasted time, money, and nerve cells (which cannot be reproduced).

### Is it wise to pay to join an affiliate program?

No. In fact, it is a sure sign that you're about to put your money into a con artist's pocket. Stay away from affiliate programs that charge affiliates to sign up.

### What do affiliate managers look at in affiliate applications?

When applying into an affiliate program you want to make sure you meet *all* of the following seven criteria:

1. Include your full name or a real company name;
2. List a working website (if for some reason it is password-protected, give the affiliate manager a demo access to see things from the inside);
3. If website categorization (as on some affiliate networks) is possible, make sure you're listed in a category that actually matches what you're doing;
4. If your website isn't in the same "niche" as the merchant's product/service, include an additional explanation on how you plan to promote them;
5. Read the program's Terms and Conditions, ensuring you comply with them even at the application stage;
6. List a working email address (and do reply back if you're asked to clarify something);

7. Avoid spelling mistakes, clichés, and nonsense descriptions of promotional methods you are planning on using to market the merchant.

If you've done all of the above, and your application still gets declined, contact the affiliate program manager. Persistence always pays off.


## Are there turn-key solutions for affiliates?

A few years ago I got an email from an affiliate that went as follows, "I'm a new affiliate and I would like to know if you know of any Turn-Key operations available at this time."

While you may certainly purchase an already functioning affiliate website and start your affiliate journey this way, I would highly recommend you start by building something *yourself*. First of all, purchasing a successful affiliate website will undoubtedly be a more expensive way to start as an affiliate. Secondly, to become a successful affiliate marketer you really want to learn things from the inside out, thereby becoming capable of exploring new niches and monetizing newly-built websites. And thirdly, "clones" have very slim chances of becoming as popular as the original.

Having said all of the above there are several solutions that can make the start of your affiliate journey significantly smoother. For example, there are products like BuildANicheStore.com, which helps you build affiliate websites as an eBay affiliate out there. Make sure you also study the lists of data feed import tools, coupon integrators, and WordPress plugins on the following pages of this book.

## Should I consider hyphenated domain names for niche websites?

When picking a domain name for your niche site (e.g., a line of sports memorabilia or an online educational course), it may make sense to look into registering a *keyword*-rich domain name for your website (e.g., EuropeanSoccerJerseys.com, OnlineEducationDegrees.net, etc.).

However, keyphrase domain names are not always available for registration. Hence, the hyphenated option question.

Some say that hyphens in domain names are a "no-no" because it is nearly impossible for people to remember to put the hyphens in, while others state that it isn't bad for your SEO at all and hyphenated domain names do well with niche search engine queries.

Some time ago I conducted an experiment, registering two domain names: both in highly competitive niches, one hyphenated another one not. The non-hyphenated one reached the #1 position on Google and MSN about a month after its registration and adding content to the website, whereas the hyphenated one did relatively well with other search engines, but wasn't very successful with Google (read: not even in the top 100 results for the target keyphrase). Based on this experience, I would recommend looking for a non-hyphenated domain name over a hyphenated one.

If, however, you do decide to go with a domain name that contains separators (such as hyphens or underscores), you want to stay away from underscores. Google, for example, is known for treating only hyphens as separators, but not underscores.

Having said all of the above, keep in mind the constantly-changing dynamic of how search engines work. For instance, between my above-quoted experiment and the publishing of this book Google had an Exact Match Domain (EMD) update aimed to ensure there is no longer a high correlation between keywords in domains and how they rank. Also, a well-developed value-adding website (even if on a hyphenated domain name or not a .com one) will always beat a poorly maintained (and/or one-page-long) websites.

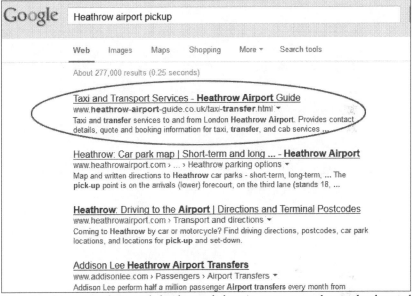

Example of how a website with hyphenated domain name outranks non-hyphenated ones, including one for Heathrow airport itself

## Is blogging a good promotional technique?

One of the best, actually! If you're an affiliate, and you are not yet blogging — you're missing out! You are missing out because you are not utilizing one of the best methods of driving targeted (or even niche) traffic to your website.

Pick a topic you're passionate and knowledgeable about, and start a blog today! It is extremely easy to do using WordPress (hosted on their server or yours) and you can get going in a matter of minutes.

Once you've started a blog, make sure you follow these 7 rules:

1. Post on it regularly (twice a week is fairly easy to stick with)
2. Write about topics that are hot/popular
3. Blog on topics in a way that adds value
4. Keep your blog post titles keyword-rich, and your blog pages SEO-friendly
5. Respond to comments made under your posts in a timely manner (this may help you create a whole social community around your blog at one point)
6. Embed social sharing buttons (to make it easy for your readers to "like" your posts on Facebook, "pin" them on Pinterest, Tweet and share them with their Google+ circles)
7. Add a forum to your blog when you have enough active visitors for them to create discussions of their own

Blogs that are updated frequently are also frequently indexed by search engines. If you stay on top of things that are important in your niche and blog in a value-added manner, you will soon gain your own audience. The Internet has removed the need for you to go to a publisher to publish your thoughts in order for them to be communicated to the world. You can start speaking to the world in a matter of minutes. And, if you do it wisely, you can also make decent money along the way too.

## What platform should I use for my blog?

Between such choices as WordPress, Typepad, Blogger, Movable Type and others, I personally prefer *WordPress*. With the abundance of themes and plugins available for this platform (free of charge or at affordable prices) WordPress blogs are easily customizable. They are also extremely user-friendly and affiliates with little or no blogging experience can start creating really beautiful (and search-engine friendly) posts in no time at all. I've worked with proprietary blogging platforms and TypePad extensively, and in my eyes WordPress wins it hands down.

According to the Pingdom's 2012 study (see www.prussakov.com/BlogStats) 48% of the world's top 100 blogs prefer WordPress.

If you decide to go with WordPress, you must go with their *self-hosted* solution because unlike other platforms WordPress doesn't allow many types of advertising (including some affiliate links) on free blogs (i.e. ones hosted on their servers). Their Advertising TOS state:

> AdSense, Yahoo, Chitika, TextLinkAds, and other third-party advertising is not allowed here at WordPress.com. ...In addition to AdSense-type ads, please do not use the following services on your blog:Sponsored or paid posts, including PayPerPost, ReviewMe, and Smorty.Affiliate or referral links to the following domains: usercash, clickbank, clickhop, cashrocks, payingcash...

Hosting a WordPress blog on your own is easy, and its installation doesn't take longer than a few minutes. You want to download the latest version of WordPress here, unpack the archive file, upload it to your server, and they will walk you through the rest of the installation process.

## What are some WordPress plugins for affiliates?

Obviously, new ones are being created/added all the time, but (in addition to data feed-related ones, which are mentioned later) the following ones are worth checking out.

- **Affiliate Link Encoder from AvantLink** – Detects and changes direct links into affiliate tracking links for the merchants that are in the AvantLink network.
- **Commission Junction Product Search** – Creates Commission Junction product listings within blog posts and pages.
- **Clickbank Widget** – Adds targeted ads for Clickbank products to your blog's sidebar.
- **LinkShare RSS DealFeed** – Automatically populates your WordPress blog with deals and other promotional content.
- **LinkShare AdMix** – Helps integrate RSS content ads from LinkShare advertisers with your blog posts.
- **Skimlinks Affiliate Marketing Tool** – Allows you to "instantly monetize untapped links on your blog."
- **123Linkit Affiliate Marketing Tool** – Transforming keywords into affiliate links.
- **Pretty Link** – Allows you to "shrink, track and share any URL on the Internet from your WordPress website" creating shortlinks "coming from your own domain." Each hit is tracked with details "of where the hit came from, the browser, OS and host."
- **Affiliate Link** – Another tool to shorten your affiliate links using your own domain name (and not any of the URL-shortening services). Tracking also provided.
- **Ad Squares Widget** – Helps you display and manage 125×125 ad square banners (and other sizes). Works "with standard affiliate ads, or even with ad network codes."
- **WP125** – A robust and popular ad management plugin for WordPress.
- **Amazon Autoposter** – Allows users to post products from Amazon.com in their own blogs (automatically, based on keyword match).
- **Amazon Product In a Post Plugin** – Help you "quickly add a formatted Amazon Product/Item to a post or page by using just the Amazon product ASIN (also known as the ISBN-10)."
- **Amazon Affiliate Link Localizer** – "Automatically changes any Amazon link on your site to use your affiliate ID" and "also changes the link to point to the user's local (i.e. country-specific) Amazon store."

- **Amazon Store** – Helps you quickly create your own Amazon affiliate store.
- **Amazon Post Purchase** – Based on the above-quoted Product In a Post plugin, but works with sidebars "in themes that support dynamic sidebars."
- **Amazon Product Link Widget** – Another sidebar widget for Amazon product links/ads.
- **WP AmaNiche** – An interesting plugin for Amazon affiliates.
- **PinRedirect** – A theme for Amazon affiliates to promote links on Pintrest

## Is participating in Google AdSense recommended for affiliates?

Among other interesting facts, the Technorati's *State of the Blogosphere 2011* report revealed that "self serve tools to offer contextual ads or pay per click ads" (which would include Google AdSense in this context) were the most popular blog monetization method (used by 60% of bloggers), followed closely by "affiliate advertising links" (used by 50%).

It isn't unusual for an affiliate to run AdSense units *simultaneously* with affiliate banners, text links, affiliate product feeds, etc.

Are these two methods *conflicting* (one being detrimental to the best performance of the other) or can they be complimentary?

I spoke with a super affiliate who split-tested the performance of web pages with affiliate links only versus those that had both affiliate links and AdSense units. It turned out that the addition of AdSense boxes did not cause *any* decrease in his affiliate revenue, but on the contrary, increased that affiliate's overall earnings by adding a new income-generating method.

It is certainly worth experimenting on your own and complimenting affiliate links with AdSense ads. Chances are you will discover that it's really not an "either... or..." situation, but a "both... and..." one.

## What are affiliate disclosures & why are they important?

On December 1, 2009 the Federal Trade Commission (FTC) enacted their "Guides Concerning the Use of Endorsements and Testimonials in Advertising." You may find the full document at FTC.gov, but in a nutshell, it explains that the FTC views merchant-affiliate relationship in a sponsor-endorser light, where the latter must disclose their relationship with the former. FTC made it clear that affiliates are not expected to include the disclosure on every page of their website. In an October 2009 interview with the *Fast Company*, the assistant director for FTC's division of advertising practices, Richard Cleland, said, "Whether you make it outside of the text but in proximity to blog, or incorporate it into the blog discussion itself — those are the issues that bloggers will have discretion about." So a dedicated Disclosure Policy page visible from every page of the website should suffice, but you *must* have one.

Additionally, on March 12, 2013 another important document was released by the FTC. It is called ".com Disclosures: How to Make Effective Disclosures in Digital Advertising" and is a must-review. You may find it at http://ftc.gov/os/2013/03/130312dotcomdisclosures.pdf.

## How should I word the disclosure & where should I place it?

The Federal Trade Commission seems to be very clear on their expectations. Addressing the question they write:

**I'm an affiliate marketer with links to an online retailer on my website. When people click on those links and buy something from the retailer, I earn a commission. What do I have to disclose? Where should the disclosure be?**

Let's assume that you're endorsing a product or service on your site and you have links to a company that pays you commissions on sales. If you disclose the relationship clearly and conspicuously on your site, readers can decide how much weight to give your endorsement. In some instances, where the link is embedded in the product review, a single disclosure may be adequate. When the product review has a clear and conspicuous disclosure of your relationship – and the reader can see both the product review and the link at the same time – readers have the information they need. If the product review and the link are separated, the reader may lose the connection.

As for where to place a disclosure, the guiding principle is that it has to be clear and conspicuous. Putting disclosures in obscure places – for example, buried on an ABOUT US or GENERAL INFO page, behind a poorly labeled hyperlink or in a terms of service agreement – isn't good enough. The average person who visits your site must be able to notice your disclosure, read it and understand it.

Source: http://bit.ly/FTCGuides-FAQs

For sample affiliate disclosures make sure to check out my http://prussakov.com/FTCdisclosure blog post.

## Is email marketing acceptable?

Absolutely! In fact, when you use self-built double opt-in (aka confirmed subscription) email lists, it is actually an extremely effective method of marketing used by many successful affiliates. So, host subscription forms on your websites, build your targeted email lists, and use them.

Two things must be mentioned here: (i) stay away from email lists for sale (build your own!), and (ii) avoid being accused of spam; always provide a working "unsubscribe"

**53**

mechanism at the end of every email you send out. Here is what SpamCop.net says about e-mails that cannot be reported as spam:

**Unsubscribing**

On January 1, 2004, the CAN-SPAM Act became law in the US. (CAN-SPAM is an acronym for **C**ontrolling the **A**ssault of **N**on-**S**olicited **P**ornography **A**nd **M**arketing). CAN-SPAM requires all unsolicited commercial email contain a label of unsolicited commercial email (although it doesn't require a particular method or label), a working unsubscribe mechanism and a physical address for the sender. It also prohibits the use of forged or falsified headers and misleading or deceptive subject lines. Many legitimate senders are complying with some or all of the provisions of the CAN-SPAM act, but so are many spammers. CAN-SPAM compliance is not necessarily a reliable way to distinguish solicited from unsolicited email. Be aware that CAN-SPAM requires that an individual be removed from a list upon request.

So even if it's a double opt-in email list, make sure you have the working "unsubscribe" mechanism in place.

## What are affiliate data feeds?

Any data feed is essentially a file (.CSV, .XML, .XLS or any other type) that lists all your product information, such as product ID, product name, description, price, stock availability, etc. The format of the affiliate data feed is normally such that the affiliate can interpret and understand it, be it with or without the help of any additional piece of software. By supplying affiliates with data feeds, merchants are aiming at enabling us to feature their products right on our websites. For this purpose besides the above-quoted pieces of information, they also include URL paths to thumbnail and larger product images, URLs leading to the pages where the individual products are featured, product categorization, and often even product-specific keywords. Affiliates may import merchant data feeds into their websites with the help of such software applications as WebMerge, online-based solutions such as PopShops, GoldenCAN and Datafeedr.com, or by possessing relevant programming skills themselves. The final goal is to present the merchant's product line on the affiliate website, giving our visitors a chance to browse, search, and view the merchant's products right on our affiliate website. The customer is transferred to the merchant website only once he/she clicks a "Buy," "More Info," "Purchase," or any other similar button on the affiliate website. That's when the affiliate cookie gets set, and should the purchase go through, a commission is made.

## What are the tools to help one work with data feeds?

I've already mentioned several data feed-import tools above, but there certainly are more. I have put together a list of 21 such tools (in the order of my personal preference), which I have seen in action and am confident of:

1. **PopShops** — Easy-to-use solution with a web interface that allows affiliates to create storefronts mixing and matching products from different merchants on different affiliate platforms.
2. **GoldenCAN** — Offers a number of easy cut-and-paste integration solutions for affiliate data feeds of multiple merchants.
3. **WebMerge** — Allows affiliates to publish data feeds "with templates from any HTML editor on any web server and then automate it."
4. **DatafeedR** — Position themselves as "a system that enables you to create and embed an affiliate store into your WordPress blog."

**5. Easy Content Units** — A U.K. equivalent of PopShops, with a price comparison option.

**6. DatafeedFile** — Borrowed GoldenCAN's concept and created a similar tool, adding a price comparison shopping functionality.

**7. Datafeed Studio** — Classic web application installable on the affiliate's server to upload affiliate data feeds, turning them into websites.

**8. FusePump** — Works with a number of (mostly UK-based) merchants helping affiliates "integrate and optimise product data feeds to maximise revenue."

**9. FeedShare** — Another interesting data feed-import tool with a variety of integration methods.

**10. Store Burst UK** — Works as a subaffiliate "network," allowing its users to create and run affiliate shops driven by data feeds.

**11. Price Tapestry** — PHP and MySQL price comparison engine based on Magic Parser, a PHP library designed for working with affiliate product feeds.

**12. Product Showcase Creator** — affSolutions' "easy to use, web-based tool that creates affiliate-link encoded product showcases in seconds."

**13. CSV Pig** — An affiliate data feed import plugin for WordPress

**14. myDatafeedScripts.com** — PHP scripts simplifying work with affiliate data feeds of major affiliate networks and individual affiliate programs.

**15. SellFire** — A newer tool which lets you "create an affiliate store for your website in minutes." They work with all major affiliate networks as well as Amazon's affiliate program.

Also, do not forget about network-based tools like the following ones (in alphabetical order):

**16. Affiliate Window's Create-a-Feed** — Part of a robust ShopWindow Toolset which allows affiliates to work with a database of several million products.

**17. AvantLink's Datafeed Manager** – The product's slogan, "customizable data feeds, updated daily," speaks for itself and this tool is definitely worth checking out.

**18. LinkShare's LinkLocator Direct** — "A Web service data feed that provides you with information on advertisers in" the network allowing you "to download different types of creative directly from the advertisers."

**19. PaidOnResults' Content Units** — A dynamic solution that allows affiliate to cut and paste a code into your website, resting assured that "the Content Unit will remain current, with the latest products... without any additional work required."

**20. ShareASale's Make-a-Page** — A feature that helps affiliates search and select products (across their merchants) and create precoded pages to thereafter cut and paste HTML code from.

**21. Webgains' iSense Ad Creator** — Allows affiliates to automatically display relevant products (or contextual ads of a kind) depending on the web page's context.

Things change nearly *daily*, so keep an eye out for new tools that become available for affiliates.

## What contextual monetization tools are available for affiliates?

If you are producing online content, or run a User-Generated Content (UGC) website like a forum for example, there are several tools that allow you to enjoy the benefits of contextual and semantic monetization without having to join individual affiliate programs. Some of the services to check out would be Skimlinks, Viglink, and Kehalim.com.

## Do I have to offer/embrace merchants' coupons?

You do not *have* to, but I highly recommend you do. You do not have to be targeting frugal shoppers to benefit from merchant's coupons and/or promos. They have proven to be a tremendous conversion booster, regardless of the audience. According to Forrester "online coupons and promotion codes positively influence the purchase cycle" [source: *The Impact Of*

*Online Coupons And Promotion Codes* report] increasing conversions for content, datafeed, paid search, and every other type of affiliates.

### What coupon integration tools should I use?

Every major affiliate network offers coupon feeds. Here are just a few examples:

- AvantLink has its Dynamic Coupon Feed
- Commission Junction has a Coupon-Only Offers RSS Feed
- LinkShare's LinkLocator is an equivalent API solution
- LinkConnector has a Coupon/Promotions Feed
- ShareASale offers a Deals Database Feed

However, in reality not all affiliates are tech-savvy enough to comfortably use the above-mentioned coupon feeds (and/or API). For those of us who aren't, there are two options: (i) hire someone to help you integrate these feeds with your website(s) or (ii) use a tool that will do it for you. Thankfully, there are a number of good tools out there. Here are just a few (in alphabetical order; with respective URLs):

- Coupilia - www.coupilia.com
- CouponFeed - www.couponfeed.net
- FeedShare - www.feedshare.com
- For Me To Coupon - www.formetocoupon.com
- GoldenCAN - www.goldencan.com
- iCodes - www.icodes-us.com
- PopShops - www.popshops.com
- Prosperent - www.prosperent.com/tools/api

## What types of deals convert best?

My experience has been that the more popular and better converting deals are dollar or percentage off coupons, free shipping deals, and discounts tied either to the number of items purchased (73% of customers go for the "Buy 2 Get 1 Free" deal offered by an ink merchant whose program we manage) or to the sale amount that qualifies the customer for a deal.

## What is the best way to contact merchants?

Merchants that care about a healthy affiliate communication channel will always list their affiliate manager's contact details right on the affiliate program page.

However, in some cases and when their affiliate program is run on an affiliate network, the network's internal messaging system (or even going through a network rep) may be a more efficient way to get a hold of them.

Also, if an affiliate program is run by an outsourced program management (OPM) agency, the agency will often answer your client-related question better and quicker than the merchant themselves. And if they don't have the answer, they will connect you with the right person within the company.

# III.
# Advanced Topics

## How do I link to specific pages?

Be it a specific product or a concrete landing page on the merchant's website, here you depend on the tools that the merchant offers – either via their in-house platform or what's available through the affiliate network(s) on which they operate.

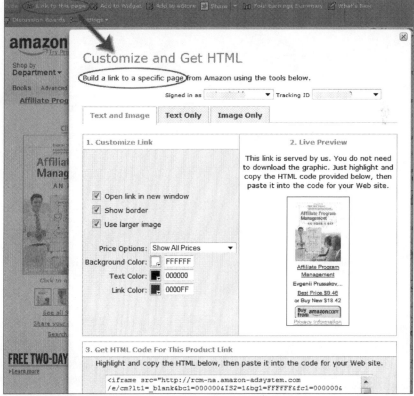

Amazon provides affiliates with a convenient deep-linking tool

Unlike a few years ago, nearly all major affiliate networks now offer deep-linking tools as well. Here are just a few to mention:

- AvantLink - Custom Link Builder
- Affiliate Window - FireAW Deeplink Builder (FireFox plugin)

- Commission Junction - Deep Link Builder (FireFox and Chrome plugins)
- eBay Enterprise Affiliate Network - ability to override set URL with custom URL
- LinkShare - LinkGenerator Bookmarklet
- Paid On Results - Deep Link Generator
- ShareASale - "Create a Custom Link" tool

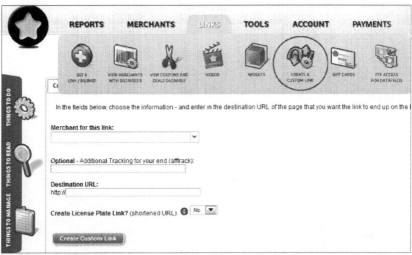

ShareASale's "Create a Custom Link" tool

## What is affiliate link cloaking?

"To cloak" is a beautiful verb that Webster's Dictionary defines as "to cover or hide with or as if with a cloak," in other words, to disguise. Link cloaking is therefore link disguising (from bots and/or humans) by hiding the actual affiliate link behind one that does not look like an affiliate URL. For example, instead of having your affiliate link to Wal-Mart.com's grills look like this,

http://linksynergy.walmart.com/fs-
bin/click?id=Qw52BwgCHiY&offerid=130155.10024349&type=3&subid=0

you may cloak it to look like something like this,

http://myownurl.com/walmart-grills

Why would you want to cloak your affiliate links? A veteran affiliate Scott Jangro once listed 5 reasons why affiliates cloak links:

1.  To make long URLs more manageable
2.  To prevent commission leaks
3.  Not to look like affiliate sites to search engines
4.  To prevent passing of "link juice"
5.  To hide links from "hijackers"

Source: http://www.jangro.com/link-cloaking/

Links may be cloaked with the help of redirectors, URL shorteners, or even WordPress plugins. At the end of the day, besides the above-mentioned reasons, you also have your own tracking of clicks on your affiliate links.

## Is affiliate link cloaking okay with search engines?

Back in 2011 in my "Is Affiliate Link Cloaking Okay with Google?" blog post I wrote:

> It all boils down to the *intent* of the cloaking. Are you trying to trick Google into believing something about your webpage that it's really not? If you are, you're asking for trouble... If you aren't, and cloaking your affiliate links to make them more manageable (and/or secure) you should be okay.

After putting it together I Tweeted to Google's Matt Cutts, asking him to correct me if I were wrong in my understanding. Matt replied:

Apparently, "cloaking" is really not the best word to describe what affiliates are predominantly doing. The better words would be URL "masking," "shortening," or "disguising."

In a 2012 Google Groups discussion on the topic, Google's John Mu confirmed:

> ...using tools like that to obfuscate your links isn't something that we'd worry about. ...Our algorithms expect unique, compelling, and high-quality content on your site. Whether you're an affiliate or not, it's important to us that users are able to find what they're looking for on your site – otherwise they might be better served by having the final destination in our search results. It doesn't matter so much that a link is an affiliate link, or where the ultimate target is (and with that in mind, it doesn't provide any additional "SEO" benefit to hide that from search engines), it's really much more about the additional value that your pages add.

Source: http://prussakov.com/LinkCloaking

So once again, unless you are "cloaking" to trick search engines, serving them different redirects (than what you would show to human visitors of your website), you are okay.

## May I charge merchants placement fees?

Sometimes in addition to the commissions, affiliates may (and do) indeed charge merchants placement fees to put up links. However, in the vast majority of cases merchants will first want to see your performance (either in form of sales, leads, clicks, or at least compelling traffic statistics from an independent tool/service).

## Do affiliates run newsletter campaigns?

Yes, and it is highly recommended that you start building your email lists right from the outset. I suggest you divide your attention between two types of newsletters: (i) one geared towards your target audience (naturally, your *primary* type of newsletter) and (ii) another one for the advertisers and affiliate managers you work with. The more successful affiliates maintain both types of email lists and corresponding newsletters.

Wondering how often is not too often to email? I recommend starting with monthly emails and experimenting with bi-monthly e-mails after some time. The key to making the newsletter(s) work for you is in delivering relevant information worthy of your audience's time and attention. If you don't have anything worthwhile to announce to them, better skip a newsletter than have them unsubscribe as a result.

## What is cookie stuffing?

Cookie stuffing, cookie dropping, forced clicks, or cookie sprinkling is a blackhat marketing method used by affiliates to set tracking cookies on the end user's machine, often without the consent of the user, and with the purpose of creating an impression that the customer/user referral is to be attributed to the blackhat affiliate's efforts.

In early 2013 two years after being indicted for cookie stuffing (which resulted in eBay Partner Network paying out over $20 million in affiliate commissions) one of the violators, Shawn Hogan, pleaded guilty to "wire fraud."

In their textbook on criminal law Thomas J. Gardner and Terry M. Anderson give a concise explanation of what exactly "wire fraud" is defining it as:

> A fraudulent scheme that uses interstate or international wire or other electronic communications.
>
> Source: *Criminal Law*, p. 484

The *United States Code* elaborates further:

> Whoever, having devised or intending to devise any scheme or artifice to defraud, or for obtaining money or property by means of false or fraudulent pretenses, representations, or promises, transmits or causes to be transmitted by means of wire, radio, or television communication in interstate or foreign commerce, any writings, signs, signals, pictures, or sounds for the purpose of executing such scheme or artifice, shall be fined under this title or imprisoned not more than 20 years, or both.
>
> Source: 18 USC Sec. 1343

Cookie stuffing is a very serious criminal offense. If you as an affiliate are already engaged in it, or are just thinking of doing it, re-read the last two lines of the USC above, and think again! It isn't worth it.

## What emerging markets should I consider?

When looking at branching out beyond your primary market, you may be recommended to look at BRIC countries

(Brazil, Russia, India, China). And while I believe affiliates should be monitoring what's happening in the online economies of these four countries, the top three countries to consider are not among these. I recommend (1) the United Kingdom, (2) Germany, and (3) France — in this order. According to the Centre for Retail Research, these three have "accounted for 71% of total European online sales" in 2012. Localize your creatives, websites (or landing pages), and partner with local experts for SEO and other help (in respective languages).

It is also worth pointing out that with localization into German and French you will not only cover Germany and France, but become open to Austria, Switzerland, French-speaking Canada, and Belgium.

Whichever market(s) you choose, keep the specifics in mind and do your due diligence *prior* to entering the market. For example, you'll want to know that in Russia unless an affiliate works via an affiliate network or incorporates locally, they will have difficulties being paid by local merchants, while in most Eastern European countries COD (cash-on-delivery) is a largely preferred method of payments.

## What is the *one* advice an affiliate should always keep in mind?

Whether you are a novice, or a seasoned pro, you must *learn to play without the ball.*

Consider the words of John Woden, the Naismith Basketball Hall of Fame coach, who once said, "Perhaps the most important part of offensive basketball is the part played by each man without the ball." Why is it so important? Because unless you play well without the ball, you don't get the ball! Krause, Meyer and Meyer wrote:

> One of the most difficult coaching tasks is to teach players to carry out actions that don't involve the basketball — the magnet of the game. An individual player on offense plays without the basketball over 80 percent of the time (*Basketball Skills & Drills*).

It is exactly the same way in affiliate marketing! Profit/commissions, which are "the magnet of the game," are often put by affiliates in front of another extremely important component of it — research and education. However, no super affiliate that I know has come to the heights they've reached without countless hours spent on diligent study, which helps one make educated decisions and avoid deadly pitfalls.

Ralph Pim, another basketball expert, wrote this about playing without the ball:

> Moving without the ball requires you to be adept at starting, stopping, faking, and changing directions. You must have excellent court awareness and vision so that you maintain the proper floor spacing with your teammates (*Winning Basketball: Techniques and Tips for Playing Better Offensive Basketball*).

While in affiliate marketing the majority of affiliates do not have teammates, the "excellent court awareness and vision" are certainly a must, and these come through staying on top of the latest developments (both in online marketing, and the vertical you're working in) and through constant self-improvement.

## What resources should I follow for further education?

Ah, I'm glad you've asked! This is a great question and one that is intact with the above-quoted advice to focus on *playing without the ball*. There are a number of "resources" out there. However, since in this field the ability to tell a good resource from a bad one translates into the difference between success and failure, let me conclude this section with a list of quality online resources to check out. Here is my list of resources for affiliates to follow in alphabetical order:

- ABestWeb forums: http://www.abestweb.com/forums/
- AffiliateBloggerPRO: http://www.affiliatebloggerpro.com
- Affiliate Marketers BootCamp: http://jamesmartell.com/
- Affiliate Summit videos: http://youtube.com/affiliatesummit
- Affilorama: http://www.affilorama.com/
- GeekCast.fm podcasts: http://geekcast.fm/
- PerformanceIN forums: http://performancein.com/forums/
- Thoughts for Affiliates section of my blog: http://prussakov.com/AffThoughts
- University of SF Advanced Affiliate Marketing certificate: http://bit.ly/USFaff

# Conclusion

The legendary Margaret Thatcher, who passed away just a few months before this book was sent to print, was known for defining success as "a mixture of having a flair for the thing that you are doing, knowing that it is not enough, that you have got to have hard work and a certain sense of purpose."

I don't know what made you pick up this book and, since you're reading these lines, eventually get to the end of it. Whether you did it out of a purely academic interest, to resolve your financial situation, to gain that long-desired freedom to do whatever you wish whenever you wish, or a combination of all of these, may the Iron Lady's advice help you achieve further heights wherever the affiliate marketing knowledge may take you next.

Work hard, stick to your goals, self-educate continuously, and you will inevitably succeed. My own professional path is testament to the fact that this recipe does work.

# Appendix:
# Affiliate's Glossary of Abbreviations

Below you will find a list of more than seventy acronyms and abbreviations with which every affiliate should be familiar. The list includes not only affiliate marketing shortenings, but also general marketing abbreviations that each affiliate should be comfortable using. I do not claim to have a complete list of acronyms and abbreviations, but this is a good basic one with which to start:

**AD** - Advertisement - May be in the form of a text, banner, flash, video or any other method that may be displayed on the Internet.

**AM** - Affiliate Manager - Person in charge of the management and organization of a company's affiliate program.

**ASP** - Active Server Pages - A Microsoft technology for dynamically-generated webpages that contain one or more scripts which are processed on a Microsoft web-server prior to the page being displayed to the end-user. The idea is somewhat similar to SSI (see below). See: www.asp.net

**ASP** - Application Service Provider - A third-party entity that distributes software applications or software-based services via a network or the Internet. Affiliate networks may be referred to as ASP's as their features are accessible over the Internet by merchants and affiliates alike. While referring to affiliate networks "ASP" may also stand for the "affiliate solution provider."

**B2B** - Business to Business - A way of exchanging products or services *or* a transaction that takes place between businesses rather than between a business and a consumer.

**B2C** - Business to Consumer - A way of exchanging products or services *or* a transaction that takes place between a business and a consumer, rather than between one business and another.

**BHO** - Browser Helper Object - A Dynamic-Link Library (DLL) that allows its developers to customize and control the end-user's Internet Explorer. BHOs have access to all events and properties of each browsing session. Parasitic behavior is often closely associated with BHOs.

**Bot** - Robot - A software application that crawls the Internet with the purpose of indexing websites and webpages.

**CAC** - Customer Acquisition Cost - The cost associated with convincing a website visitor to become a customer for your product/service.

**CB** - Callback - A way of interviewing somebody after a product usage. The term may also refer to any repeated attempt to contact a potential responder after an unsuccessful first-contact attempt.

**CGI** - Common Gateway Interface - A way of transferring information between an Internet server and a CGI program. CGI programs are also often referred to as *scripts* and may be written in such programming languages as C, C++, Java and Perl.

**CJ** - Commission Junction Affiliate Network - One of the major affiliate networks today. CJ has presence in the US, UK, Germany, France and Sweden. See: www.cj.com

**CPA** - Cost Per Action - Also sometimes de-abbreviated as Cost Per Acquisition, this is a payment model where an advertiser pays for each qualifying action made by the end-user in response to an as. Such qualifying actions normally fall into one of these categories: (i) sales, (ii) completions of registration or other website forms, (iii) confirming the end-user's interest in the advertiser's product/service.

**CPC** - Cost Per Click - A payment model where an advertiser pays for each click on an online Ad.

**CPI** - Cost Per Interview - General marketing term calculated as the full number of completed interviews divided by the budget allocated for the interviewing project.

**CPL** - Cost Per Lead - A payment model where an advertiser pays for each new qualifying lead. Examples of leads: (i) e-mail addresses, (ii) completed surveys, (iii) various online forms. This payment model is normally tied to the completeness and verification of the leads.

**CPM** - Cost Per Thousand - Cost per *mil* or one thousand impressions (or showings). May imply anything from the amount charged per 1000 banner impressions to a copy of a newsletter sent to 1000 subscribers.

**CPO** - Cost Per Order - A payment model where an advertiser pays for each new qualifying order.

**CPS** - Cost Per Sale - Total advertising expense divided by the total number of sales received as a result of such investment. The result of mathematical operation helps merchants determine the cost that has to be incurred to make each sale possible.

**CR** - Conversion Rate/Ratio - The percentage of visitors that take the desired action (purchase, subscription, form completion, etc.).

**CRA** - Customer Relationship Analysis/Analytics - The processing of data about customers and their relationships with the merchant in order to improve the company's future sales/services and lower cost.

**CRM** - Customer Relationship Management - Improving customer service and general interaction with customers by means of relevant methodologies and software applications geared at bettering customer understanding and increasing customer satisfaction and loyalty.

**CSS** - Cascading Style Sheets - A relatively new data format that when added to HTML, helps separate style from structure. It gives both web-developers and end-users of websites more control over how webpages are displayed and reduces HTML file sizes. Using CSS web-designers and end-users may create style sheets that determine how such elements as headers and links appear. The style sheets may then be applied to any webpage. *Cascading* refers to the fact that multiple style sheets may be applied to the same webpage.

**CTR** - Click-Through Rate/Ratio - A metrics used to measure response to advertising. CTR reflects the percentage of website visitors that click on a particular link. This percentage is obviously calculated based on the average number of click-throughs per 100 ad impressions.

**DLL** - Dynamic-Link Library - Defined by Microsoft as "an executable file that allows programs to share code and other resources necessary to perform particular tasks."

**DPSC** - Dynamic Product Showcase Creator - A tool created by AffSolutions that allows affiliates to generate a Javascript code which retrieves a merchant's product information that affiliates may then insert into their website. The code enables affiliate tracking and real-time updating of product information (AffSolutions also have static Product Showcase Creator for several merchants). This works only for merchants subscribed to this service. The full list of these merchants may be found at www.afftools.com/psc/directory.html

**DTM** - Direct To Merchant (Linking) - Linking affiliate paid search ads directly to the advertiser's website (through affiliate links).

**EPC** - Earnings Per Click - Average affiliate program's payout per one hundred clicks. This metric is one of the key ones used by affiliates to determine how attractive and promising an affiliate program is. To calculate their EPC, affiliates divide the total number of clicks by their total earnings. Such simple calculation gives them their earnings per click.

**EPM** - Earning Per Thousand - Earnings per mil or one thousand link impressions.

**FFA** - Free-For-All (Link Lists) - Lists of hyperlinks where anyone can add a link back to their website, not having to abide by any qualifications.

**GAN** - Google Affiliate Network - Affiliate network, originally known as Doubleclick Performics, acquired by Google in 2007, but closed on July 31, 2013.

**IM** - Instant messaging - A way of instant text communication between two or more people via an offline or an online-based application. IM may also stand for *Instant message* or an *Instant messenger*. The most popular instant messengers today are: AIM (AOL instant messenger), YIM (Yahoo! instant messenger), MSN messenger, and one of the pioneers of the industry, ICQ. Skype has an IM imbedded in their application and allows not only for voice communication, but also for instant messaging. Instant messengers are excellent for staying in touch with your affiliates worldwide.

**LS** - Linkshare Affiliate Network - One of the leading affiliate networks in the world. In 2012 rebranded as Rakuten LinkShare to encompass LinkShare's parent company, Rakuten. See: www.linkshare.com

**MLM** - Multi-Level Marketing - A sales system within which salespeople not only receive commission on their own sales, but also smaller commission on the sales of the people they convince to become sellers. Such multi-tier programs are generally not welcomed in the affiliate marketing community and have nothing to do with traditional affiliate marketing.

**OPM** - Outsourced Affiliate (Program) Manager - Affiliate manager that perform program management outside the company's premises.

**ODP** - Open Directory Project - The largest human edited directory on the Internet. Google and thousands of other websites are using its data throughout the web. Sometimes also referred to as DMOZ.

**PFI** - Pay For Inclusion - Also sometimes abbreviated as PPI (or Pay Per Inclusion), it is a search engine marketing model in which website owners pay a search engine to be listed in search results. Some search engines support it not distinguishing between paid listings and organically achieved search rankings, while others label PFI listings as hidden advertising, demanding paid search results to be clearly marked as an ad.

**PFP** - Pay For Performance - An Internet marketing model based on delivering sales or other measurable performance.

**PJX** – PepperJam Exchange - One of the major affiliate networks. In July 2013 rebranded as the eBay Enterprise Affiliate Network. See: www.ebayenterprise.com/marketing_solutions/affiliate_netw ork/

**PM** - Private Message - An internal forum or other online community means of communication between the members of the forum/community.

**POP** - Point-Of-Purchase - The location where the product/service is actually purchased. May refer to both a physical location or to the online equivalent.

**POS** - Point-Of-Sale - Same as POP.

**PPA** - Pay Per Action - Another way to refer to a CPA model (see above).

**PPC** - Pay Per Click - An Internet marketing model in which website owners pay only for targeted clicks. Where search engines' PPC campaigns are concerned, you pay only for clicks coming from searchers looking for the keywords that you bid on. The main providers of such models are Google (Google Adwords) and Yahoo! Marketing (Overture). The British Internet also has such large providers as Espotting.

**PPCSE** - Pay Per Click Search Engine - Search engine that supports PPC campaigns, allowing for the search results to be ranked according to the bid amount received. Advertisers are charged according to the classic PPC pattern – or only for the clicks occurred.

**PPI** - Pay Per Impression - An Internet marketing model in which payment is calculated based on the number of impressions an Ad receives.

**PPL** - Pay Per Lead - An Internet marketing model in which payment is due only when qualifying *leads* are received by the advertiser.

**PPS** - Pay Per Sale - An Internet marketing model in which payment is due only when qualifying *sales* are received by the advertiser/merchant.

**PR** - PageRank™ - Google's patented method for ranking webpages based on a complex technology (see: www.google.com/technology) that weighs each webpage on a numerical scale of 0 to 10. The purpose of such measuring consists in defining the relevance and importance of any given webpage within the set of the webpages it is hyperlinked with. Google's PR of a webpage has an immediate effect on organic ranking of the latter in search engines.

**PSC** - Product Showcase Creator - Static version of AffSolutions' Dynamic Product Showcase Creator

**PV** - Pageview - There are two ways to define a pageview, depending on the context. One defines it as a single webpage viewed by a web-user through a browser. The other one characterizes every file which either has a text file suffix (.html, .text), or which is a directory index file as pageview. The latter definition helps estimate the number of authentic documents transmitted by the server, which is helpful for website statistics. Images, CGI scripts, Java applets, or any other HTML objects (except all files ending with one of the pre-defined pageview suffixes, such as .html or .text) are not considered pageviews.

**ROI** - Return On Investment - Originally a finance term, it reflects a measure of a company's profitability. It is equal to a fiscal year's income divided by common stock and preferred stock equity, plus long-term debt. In the investment and business analytics world, the ROI measures how effectively the investment is used to generate profit. In e-commerce, the term retains its financial sense, but more often than not, its definition is simplified to the evaluation of the money earned (or lost) against the amount of money invested.

**RON** - Run Of Network - An online advertising term that designates a type of Internet promotion where banners, images, media, or text ads appear on a network of websites.

**ROS** - Run Of Site - An online advertising term that is defined as a type of Internet promotion where banners, images, media, or text ads appear on a webpages within one website.

**RSS** - Real Simple Syndication *previously* Rich Site Summary - A file format originally developed by Netscape. On the one hand, it allows webmasters to put the content of their sites into a standardized format (an XML file called an RSS feed, webfeed, RSS stream or RSS channel); on the other hand, it lets users subscribe to their favorite websites and view/ organize the content through RSS-aware software applications. As such, RSS provides a way for websites to dispense their content outside of a web browser. The RSS technology has basically provided the world with a better technique for users to automatically stay updated on their favorite websites. RSS supports news feeds, events listings, news stories, headlines, project updates, excerpts from online forums, and even corporate information.

**SAS** - Shareasale Affiliate Network - One of the leading present-day affiliate networks. Known for its stance against parasites, its strive for transparency, and its strong affiliate support. See: www.shareasale.com

**SE** - Search Engine - A program developed to search for documents by keywords and key phrases. Each request returns a list of the documents where the requested keyword or key phrase is found. Examples: Google.com, Yahoo.com

**SEM** - Search Engine Marketing - Marketing acts associated with researching, submitting, and positioning a website within search engines with an aim at achieving the best website exposure on these search engines. The best exposure may be achieved by improving the website's search engine ranking, participating in PPC campaigns or a combination of these and other relative activities (for example, SEO).

**SEMPO** - Search Engine Marketing Professional Organization - A non-profit organization established to increase people's awareness of the value of search engine marketing through continuous education.

**SEO** - Search Engine Optimization - Acts associated with website altering with an aim of achieving higher website rankings on major search engines.

**SEP** - Search Engine Positioning - Acts aimed at achieving higher *organic* (natural) rankings on major search engines.

**SERP** - Search Engine Results Page - The page displayed to the end-user after submitting the search query.

**SID** - Shopper ID - A parameter that affiliates may add to their tracking URL's to be able to monitor which links produced which sales and/or leads. SID affiliate tracking was originally invented by Commission Junction (see www.cj.com/downloads/smartrewards.pdf), but it is now also offered by every major affiliate network, as well as by some providers of in-house software. The acronym is also sometimes spelled out as a *session ID*. I believe the time has come to broaden its meaning into a unified *Sub ID* which would include CJ's *sid*, DirectTrack's *dp*, LinkShare's *u1*, MyAffiliateProgram's *sub*, Performics' *mid*, ShareASale's *afftrack*, and other link parameters carrying out the same function.

**SMB** - Small and Medium-Sized Businesses - The abbreviation is used interchangeably with an SME shortening, which stands for small and medium enterprises. In the European Union, enterprises with fewer than 50 employees are categorized as "small," while those that employ fewer than 250 workers are considered "medium." In the United States, conversely, "small" businesses refer to those with fewer than 100 employees, while "medium" designates businesses with fewer than 500 persons employed. An interesting fact is that over 90% of all American businesses fall under the US definition of "small business."

**SSI** - Server-Side Include - A variable value (e.g. a page "last updated" date) that a server can include in an HTML file before sending it to the end-user that browses the website.

**SWOT** - SWOT Analysis - A strategic planning tool aimed at singling out Strengths, Weaknesses, Opportunities and Threats in the object of study, arriving at an action plan for the proper use of the collected data. SWOT is an excellent way to analyze any marketing or management endeavor, affiliate programs included. The SWOT matrix essentially consists of four quadrants. Each of the quadrants helps the researcher analyze where the object of his/her study is now, where it is wanted to be, and how to get there.

**TOS** - Terms Of Service - Rules and regulations that one must agree to and follow in order to use a service. In the context of affiliate marketing, the TOS acronym is frequently used to designate either an affiliate program's agreement with affiliates, or an affiliate network's service agreement.

**UBE** - Unsolicited Bulk E-mail - E-mail messages sent to the recipient as a part of a larger group of messages, all of which have essentially identical content, and are sent out without prior recipient's permission. In short, UBE stands for e-mail spam. An e-mail message may be classified as spam only if it is *both* unsolicited and bulk. Not to be accused of UBE's, affiliates should be careful in the wording of the messages sent out.

**UGC** - User-Generated Content - Various kinds of media content produced on a website by its users. Also known as CGM (consumer generated media) and UCC (user-created content).

**URL** - Uniform Resource Locator - The global address of an Internet resource on the World Wide Web (e.g., http://www.amnavivator.com)

**UV** - Unique Visitor - A term frequently used in tracking website's traffic and designating a person that visits a website more than once within a specified period of time. Traffic tracking software normally distinguishes between visitors that only visit the website once and UVs that return to the site. UVs are different from hits or page views, both of which reflect the number of documents requested from the website. UVs are often determined by the number of unique IP addresses that the site visits come from.

Made in the USA
Lexington, KY
05 October 2014